This is my digger

Written by Chris Oxlade
Photography by Christine Lalla

FRANKLIN WATTS
LONDON•SYDNEY

This edition 2009

Franklin Watts
338 Euston Road
London NW1 3BH

Franklin Watts Australia
Hachette Children's Books
Level 17/207 Kent Street
Sydney NSW 2000

Editor: Jennifer Schofield
Designer: Jemima Lumley
Photography: Christine Lalla
Digger driver: Andy Cook

Acknowledgements:
The Publisher would like to thank Karen Ross, Andy Cook
and all at Diggerland for their help in producing this book.

A CIP catalogue record for this book
is available from the British Library.

ISBN: 978 0 7496 8917 9
Dewey Classification: 629.225

Printed in China

Franklin Watts is a division of Hachette Children's Books,
an Hachette Livre UK company.
www.hachettelivre.co.uk

Contents

My digger and me

Hello! I am a digger driver.
This is the digger that I drive.

My digger digs holes and picks up soil and rubble.

Digger power

This is my digger's engine.
It makes all the parts work.

The engine is under the cover.
It is big and powerful.

This is the fuel tank.
The engine needs fuel
to work.

Digger tracks

My digger has two tracks that move it backwards and forwards.

The tracks are made from thick, tough rubber.

The tracks are very wide to stop the digger from sinking into mud.

Boom and bucket

The boom makes the digging bucket move up and down.

bucket

boom

> *The bucket has teeth that dig into the ground.*

Rams move the boom up and down. They are like muscles that push and pull, just like in your arm.

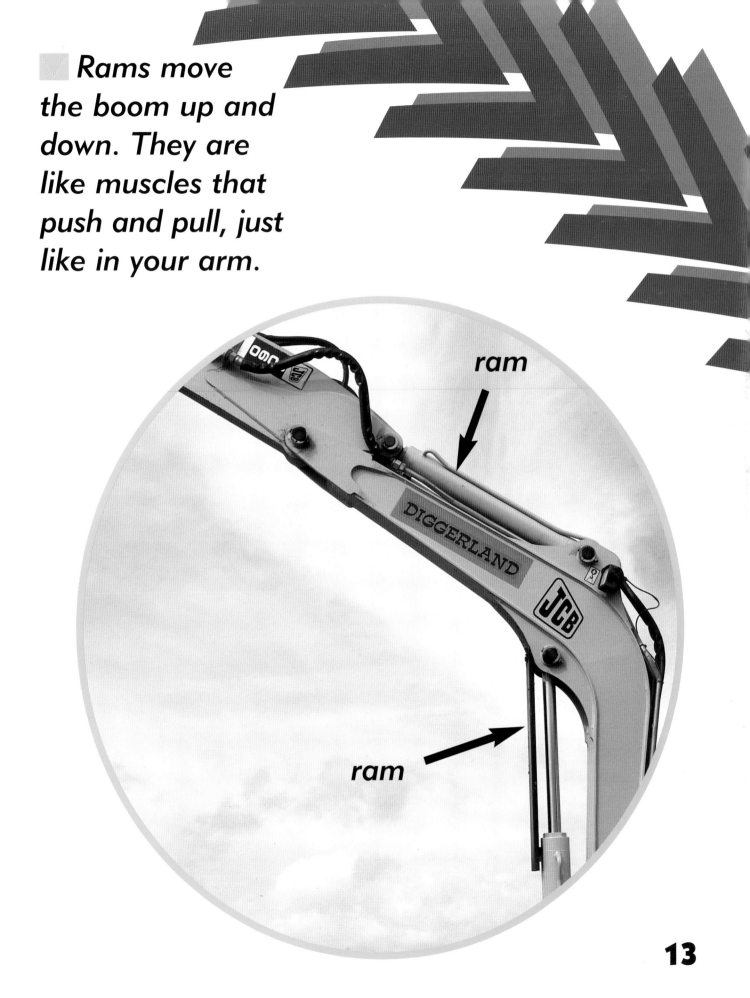

ram

ram

Digger tools

I can put other tools onto the boom instead of the digging bucket.

A hammer breaks up rock and concrete.

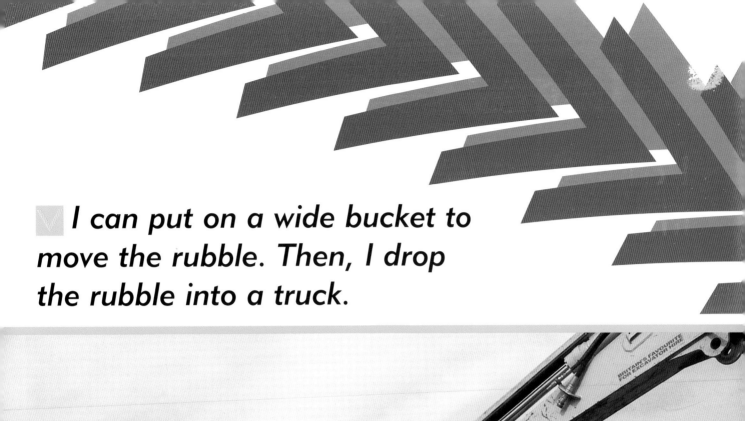

I can put on a wide bucket to move the rubble. Then, I drop the rubble into a truck.

In my cab

I sit in the cab to drive my digger.
The cab keeps me warm and dry.

The seat is comfortable and it is heated on cold days!

I can see the digger tools working through the big windows.

Digger controls

I drive the digger with pedals, levers and switches.

The foot pedals make the tracks go forwards and backwards.

Hand levers work the boom and bucket. They also make the digger's body swing round.

Digging a hole

Today, my first job is to dig a hole on a building site.

I make the bucket dig into the soil.

Then, I lift the bucket up and swing the body round.

I tip the bucket up to make the soil fall out.

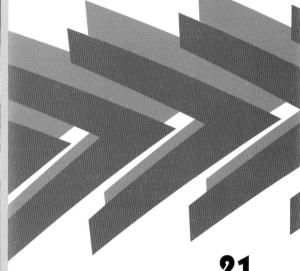

Breaking rocks

Now, I am using a bigger digger to break rocks and load a truck.

I am breaking up the rocks with the digger's hammer.

Then, I put a wide bucket onto the arm.

I use the bucket to load the rubble into a truck.

23

More diggers

Here are some more diggers that I drive.

This digger is called a backhoe loader. I use it to dig holes, lift heavy things and to move rubble.

I use this mini digger on pavements and in gardens.

Be a digger driver

It takes lots of practice
to become a digger driver.

You have to learn how to drive the digger safely around a building site.

You have to learn what all the digger's levers, pedals and switches do.

You have to learn how to use all the different digger tools.

Digger parts

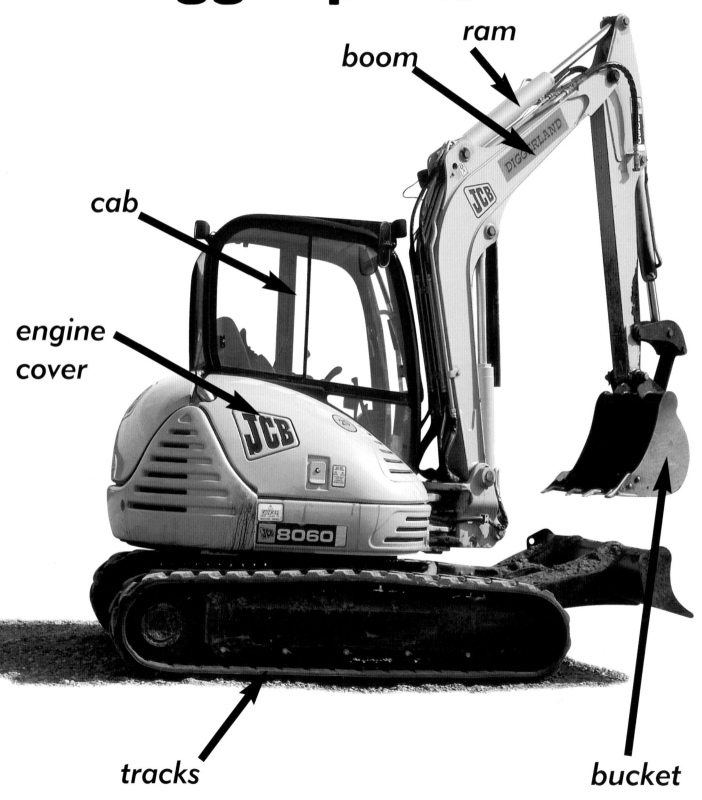

ram

boom

cab

engine cover

bucket

tracks

Word bank

body – the main part of a digger

building site – the place where a building is built

concrete – stone used in buildings

engine – the part of a digger that makes it move

fuel – the liquid that burns inside an engine

mini – small

rubble – pieces of stone

tools – the things, such as buckets and hammers, that are added to a digger to do different jobs

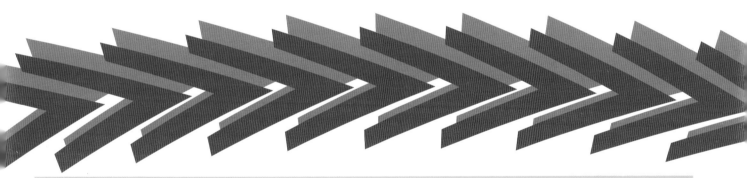

Web fun

Look at JCB's children's website for loads of digger fun: www.jcb.com/(wpjfrg45paq2ju55udsxlmyp)/jcbjunior/index.aspx

Index